CW01064483

Original title:
Lessons in Love

Author: Paula Raudsepp
ISBN HARDBACK: 978-9916-89-040-0
ISBN PAPERBACK: 978-9916-89-041-7
ISBN EBOOK: 978-9916-89-042-4

A Journey of Unspoken Promises

In shadows cast by soft moonlight,
We tread on paths our hearts have known.
Each step whispers a silent vow,
In the stillness, our souls have grown.

The winds carry words yet unspoken,
Across the fields where dreams may play.
With every heartbeat, trust is woven,
A tapestry of love's sweet sway.

Through valleys deep and mountains high,
Together we face the rising dawn.
With each glance, our spirits soar,
A journey where old fears are gone.

Underneath the starry sky,
We find our way, hand in hand.
In the quiet, time stands still,
Our promises, a gentle strand.

As the sun dips below the edge,
New tomorrows beckon us near.
With every moment, faith we pledge,
In this journey, forever clear.

Discoveries in Each Other's Eyes

In your gaze, a world unfolds,
A hidden tale in every glance.
Reflections dance like flickering gold,
Inviting hearts to join the dance.

With every blink, new stories bloom,
A universe in colors bright.
In silence shared, we banish gloom,
And find our way through the soft light.

The mysteries that lie between,
A spark of hope, a fleeting dream.
Within your eyes, I glimpse the unseen,
A depth profound as a flowing stream.

Every eyelash, a path to know,
The secrets of our souls entwined.
In each moment, love's seed we sow,
Two hearts united, gently aligned.

Together we unravel space,
Discoveries in shadows cast.
In your eyes, I find my place,
With you, I want this love to last.

The Balance of Togetherness

In harmony, we find our tune,
Like melodies in the morning light.
With every note, our hearts commune,
Creating warmth that feels so right.

The gentle push, the tender pull,
Like tides that kiss the sandy shore.
In balance struck, we are made whole,
In love's embrace, forevermore.

Through trials faced and laughter shared,
We navigate both joy and strife.
With every moment, we are paired,
A dance of hearts, a dance of life.

In quietude, our spirits blend,
With every breath, we grow, we lean.
Together, on this path, we wend,
In balance, love's bright light is seen.

Hand in hand, we face the storms,
Unified against the cold.
In each other, warmth transforms,
Together, our stories unfold.

The Heart's Lingering Echo

Whispers of love in the evening glow,
An echo that time cannot fade.
In every heartbeat, emotions flow,
A melody softly played.

Each glance shared, a lingering trace,
A memory etched upon the heart.
In tender touch, we find our space,
As two worlds merge, never apart.

Beneath the stars, shadows dance,
The night air filled with our sighs.
In every moment, a fleeting chance,
To capture love that never dies.

Through fields of gold and summer's breath,
The heart speaks louder than the rest.
In echoes soft, even in death,
Our spirits wear love's vibrant vest.

With every dawn, new promises rise,
In beauty wrapped, we rise again.
A timeless truth beneath the skies,
The heart's echo shall always remain.

Footprints in the Sand of Time

Footprints left upon the shore,
Whispers of dreams, tales of yore.
The tide rolls in, they wash away,
Yet memories linger, night and day.

With every wave, a story told,
Time dances on, both young and old.
A journey marked, yet hard to trace,
Each step we take, a sacred place.

Through storms and sun, we carry on,
In the silence, love is drawn.
Footprints fade, but hearts will bind,
In each echo, we seek to find.

Shadows fade, the sun will rise,
Hope renews beneath the skies.
In every grain, a life unfolds,
In footprints soft, our story holds.

Secrets Shared in the Night

Beneath the stars, where dreams take flight,
We whisper secrets, soft and light.
The moon, our witness, shines so bright,
In shadowed corners, bonds ignite.

Each thought exchanged, a gentle breeze,
In intimate moments, hearts at ease.
Bound by trust, we take our stand,
Hand in hand, we make our plans.

Let's chase the echoes, near and far,
Find hidden truths beneath the scar.
In twilight's hush, two souls define,
The tapestry of love, divine.

With every sigh, our stories weave,
In noonday glow, we dare believe.
Secrets shared in the softest night,
Unfold like petals, pure and bright.

Sunsets and New Horizons

The sun dips low, in hues of gold,
A canvas painted, visions bold.
Each sunset whispers a soft goodbye,
As day gives way to the evening sky.

New horizons beckon with a smile,
A promise of journeys, mile by mile.
With hopeful hearts, we gather dreams,
In twilight's glow, life softly gleams.

The stars awaken, dreams take charge,
Each twinkle speaks of life at large.
In every end, a brand new start,
Nature's rhythm, a work of art.

Let's chase the dusk, where shadows play,
And find our path in the fading day.
In every sunset lies the chance,
For new beginnings, life's sweet dance.

Hearts Entwined in Harmony

In silent whispers, hearts entwine,
A dance of souls, a bond divine.
With every glance, emotions flow,
In tender beats, our love will grow.

Like gentle streams that merge as one,
Two melodies, now softly spun.
Through trials faced, we stand as three,
In love's embrace, we seek to be.

In laughter shared, in tears we find,
The strength of hearts that are aligned.
With gentle touch, we mend the scars,
In harmony, we reach for stars.

Together strong, we face the night,
In every shadow, we find the light.
Our hearts entwined, forever free,
In perfect harmony, just you and me.

The Atlas of Hidden Sentiments

In shadows deep, where silence sways,
The heart's map hides in soft delays.
Whispers of love, like secrets penned,
Charting paths where dreams contend.

Beneath the stars, the echoes play,
Invisible threads in night's ballet.
A gaze, a touch, the spaces bloom,
Navigating through unseen rooms.

Memories linger, artfully frayed,
In the attic of thoughts, softly laid.
Every sigh a tender mark,
Guiding home through shadows dark.

Each heartbeat writes, each pulse a line,
In this atlas, where feelings entwine.
Lost in the ink of unspoken tales,
Finding meaning in gentle gales.

So hold the map, though paths may twist,
In every feeling, something missed.
With every step, a world to create,
In the atlas that love can narrate.

Grace in Every Misstep

In stumble's dance, we find our stride,
With every fall, the heart's wide.
A gentle laugh, a whispered cheer,
In missteps clear, we gather near.

Unraveled dreams can teach us more,
Than perfectly planned and sleek decor.
Through tangled roots, we rise anew,
Each misstep leads to truth in view.

Like autumn leaves that swirl and fly,
Grace in the chaos of the sky.
Embracing flaws, we learn to see,
The beauty born of irony.

A falter here, a question tossed,
In every stumble, we gain what's lost.
With open hearts, we twirl around,
In missteps sweet, our joy is found.

So let us dance through life's surprise,
With humble hearts and joyful eyes.
In every fall, there's strength to lend,
Grace is the light that will not bend.

A Song of Unfinished Conversations

In twilight's glow, the voices break,
Words linger soft, yet boldly shake.
Promises hang, like stars in flight,
In the silence of the night.

Frayed edges tell of tales untold,
In whispered dreams, the feelings fold.
Each phrase hangs heavy in the air,
An echo of thoughts we meant to share.

Threads of longing weave the past,
Memories flicker, shadows cast.
Unfinished thoughts like songs that weave,
Through moments held, we still believe.

What ifs linger in the space,
In every pause, a sweet embrace.
Each syllable, a gentle plea,
In unfinished words, we seek to be.

So let us dance in this refrain,
In lines unspoken, love remains.
In every breath of night's caress,
A song unfolds in tenderness.

Breath of Connection

In silence we hear the whispers,
Threads of thoughts weave through air.
A gaze, a nod, a gentle touch,
Binding hearts with love's soft care.

The world fades to a quiet hum,
As souls dance in a sacred space.
Together we breathe, as one,
Embracing life with sweet grace.

In laughter shared, the bond deepens,
With every moment, truth unfolds.
A symphony of hearts and voices,
In unity, a story told.

The warmth of hands intertwined,
In storms, we find steady ground.
In the pulse of connection felt,
A deeper meaning is found.

So let us treasure this magic,
The gift of knowing, side by side.
In each breath, a love unspoken,
Together forever, our stride.

Galaxies Spun from Shared Dreams

In twilight's glow, our visions spark,
Whispers of hope paint the skies.
Galaxies born from our desires,
As starlight dances in our eyes.

We weave our dreams with silken threads,
Binding truths that years unfold.
In the tapestry of aspirations,
Stories of courage, yet untold.

Through starlit paths, we wander wide,
Chasing shadows, seeking light.
In every heartbeat, galaxies grow,
In every tear, the stars ignite.

Together we soar with daring hearts,
Across the cosmos, hand in hand.
In the vastness of life's design,
Shared dreams, like stars, brightly stand.

And when the night wraps us in peace,
We'll glance at the sky, know we're free.
For in every dream we hold together,
Lives the essence of you and me.

A Score of Unfinished Symphonies

In the quiet room, melodies play,
Notes of longing, a soft refrain.
Each pause echoes with unsung songs,
A dance of hope, love, and pain.

We scribble thoughts on empty sheets,
Lyrics woven from hidden fears.
In whispers, our hearts compose the score,
While time carries away our years.

Together, we write our symphonies,
With vibrant chords of passion bright.
In perfect harmony, we create,
A symphony born from the night.

Yet some notes linger, lost in space,
Awaiting hands to guide them home.
In unfinished tunes, we find our hearts,
In the silence, our spirits roam.

So let us sing, though verses wait,
In every heartbeat, music flows.
For the beauty lies in the journey,
In the songs that life bestows.

The Softness of Understanding

In gentle murmurs, we discover,
The tender threads that bind our souls.
With open hearts, we find each other,
In the spaces, where silence rolls.

A listening ear, a caring smile,
In vulnerability, love unfolds.
We share our truths, no need for masks,
In the warmth of trust, a bond molds.

Through storms of words, we navigate,
With kindness, we weather the strife.
In the soft glow of understanding,
We embrace the beauty of life.

We learn to dance in quiet moments,
Finding solace in the storms we face.
In shared breaths, we cultivate peace,
In the heart's garden, love leaves its trace.

So let us cherish this sweet embrace,
For in understanding, we are whole.
A journey woven from heart to heart,
In the softness, we find our role.

Whispers of the Heart

In the quiet of the night,
Soft murmurs fill the air.
Hearts beat in rhythm,
As secrets they share.

Stars blink in response,
To love's gentle call.
Whispers dance around,
Binding us, one and all.

Promises linger here,
In shadows and light.
Echoes of whispers,
Guide us through the night.

Gentle sighs of dreams,
Carried on the breeze.
A tapestry of hopes,
Woven with such ease.

Listen to the silence,
It speaks without sound.
In whispers of the heart,
True love can be found.

Echoes of Affection

In the warmth of your gaze,
I find my solace.
Every glance, a promise,
Wrapped in tenderness.

Laughter rolls like waves,
Crashing on the shore.
In moments shared,
We are forevermore.

Soft touches linger,
Like shadows that play.
Each heartbeat echoes,
In a sacred ballet.

Time stands still for us,
In this tender space.
Every echo sings,
Love's immortal grace.

As sunset paints the sky,
With hues of delight.
Echoes of affection,
Shine through the night.

Tides of Tenderness

The moon pulls the sea,
With a gentle embrace.
Tides shift and flow,
In this loving space.

Waves whisper softly,
Carrying secrets near.
In their rolling rhythm,
I hold you so dear.

Sand slips through fingers,
Yet love stays constant.
In the tides of kindness,
Our dreams are abundant.

Each time the tide rises,
My heart beats in time.
For in this ocean,
Love's the perfect rhyme.

As the shoreline embraces,
The vast, open sea.
Tides of tenderness,
Will always be free.

The Art of Letting Go

In the stillness of dawn,
I release the past.
Memories float like leaves,
In the autumn blast.

With each breath I take,
The weight starts to lift.
Letting go is a gift,
A bittersweet shift.

Like clouds on a breeze,
Thoughts wander and fade.
In the art of letting,
A new path is laid.

Change dances around,
With every sunrise.
Embracing the moment,
I open my eyes.

The heart learns to mend,
In the space of goodbye.
The art of letting go,
Helps the spirit fly.

The Path of Woven Dreams

In twilight's hush, we walk this way,
Each step a whisper, come what may.
Beneath the stars, our hopes take flight,
Guiding us softly through the night.

Threads of silver weave our fates,
Entwined in stories, love awaits.
With every heartbeat, we connect,
In dreams we share, we are perfect.

The winding road bends with grace,
Where every stumble finds its place.
In laughter's echo, fears subside,
Together always, side by side.

The sun will rise, our journey true,
In morning light, renew anew.
With hope as our gentle guide,
We'll face the world, hearts open wide.

So take my hand, we'll roam afar,
Through whispered dreams, we'll find our star.
In every moment, laughter beams,
We'll walk together, chase our dreams.

Lingering Notes of Connection

In silent moments, we connect,
Like notes that linger, they reflect.
A gentle touch, a knowing glance,
In melodies, we find our dance.

The laughter shared, a timeless song,
In harmony, where we belong.
Through ups and downs, the music plays,
Our souls entwined in countless ways.

In whispers soft, our stories blend,
A symphony that knows no end.
Each heartbeat notes the love we share,
A song of hope, beyond compare.

So hold me close, let worries fade,
In this sweet serenade we've made.
Together, dear, our spirits rise,
In every note, a new surprise.

Until the stars begin to fade,
We'll dance to dreams that we have laid.
In lingering notes, we find our way,
A connection deep that will not sway.

The Compass of Kindness

In every heart, a compass lies,
Guiding us through lows and highs.
With every act of gentle grace,
We light the world in warm embrace.

A smile exchanged, a hand extended,
In kindness shown, our fears upended.
With every word, a seed we sow,
In fields of love, our spirits grow.

The compass spins, directing right,
Towards a future shining bright.
No act too small to make a change,
In kindness' path, we rearrange.

So share your heart, let kindness flow,
In every moment, let it grow.
For in the world, where darkness creeps,
Our kindness shines, our promise keeps.

Together on this journey true,
With every step, we'll see it through.
A compass of kindness to our side,
In each other, we will abide.

Among the Pages of Us

Among the pages, stories dwell,
In whispered words, we weave a spell.
Each chapter tells of joys and fears,
In ink of laughter, love, and tears.

Through twists and turns, our tales entwine,
In every line, our hearts align.
With every bookmark, moments freeze,
In the book of life, it's you and me.

The plot unfolds, with lessons learned,
As each page turns, new fires burned.
A tale of friendship, strong and true,
In every word, I find you too.

So let us write on pages wide,
With joy and love, we'll turn each tide.
Our story's rich, with colors bright,
In the book of us, eternal light.

For every ending, new begins,
In the pages, love always wins.
Together, dear, we'll craft our tale,
Among the pages, we'll prevail.

Threads of Connection

In laughter shared, our spirits weave,
A tapestry of trust we conceive.
Each moment stitched with gentle care,
A bond unbroken, always there.

Through whispered words, we bridge the gap,
In silence, find the warmest lap.
In every glance, a story told,
A friendship crafted, bright and bold.

We stitch the seams of joy and pain,
In sunny days or pouring rain.
Together strong, our hearts entwined,
In every thread, our souls aligned.

With threads of gold that shimmer bright,
We paint our journey, pure delight.
In every challenge, side by side,
This fabric of life, our hearts abide.

So let us cherish every tie,
With open hearts, we dare to fly.
In each connection, we shall find,
The strength to leave our fears behind.

Beneath the Surface of Desire

In shadows deep, our secrets hide,
A yearning flame we can't abide.
With whispers soft, we dare to dream,
In passion's dance, we lose our theme.

What lies beneath the calm facade?
A sea of wishes, love untrod.
With every glance, a spark ignites,
Awakening the hidden nights.

The heartbeats echo, wild and free,
In tangled moments, you and me.
Our longing grows like tides that swell,
Beneath the surface, stories dwell.

Let's dive into the depths unknown,
Where truths collide and love has grown.
In every sigh, a world unfolds,
In secret places, desires bold.

So let us strip away the layers,
In honesty, the heart declares.
With every heartbeat, raw and real,
We touch the truth, our souls reveal.

The Dance of Understanding

In each step shared, we learn to see,
The rhythm flows in harmony.
With open hearts, we grasp the tune,
In silent whispers, we commune.

Our thoughts entwined in gentle sway,
As shadows fade and light leads the way.
In every twirl, we bridge the gap,
A sacred bond, a loving map.

With eyes that meet in deep embrace,
We find our truth in time and space.
In every fall, a chance to lift,
Together bound, we share this gift.

Through trials faced and laughter shared,
In trusting hands, we've always dared.
The dance of life, a gracious turn,
In every step, a flame to burn.

So let us move with grace and ease,
In unity, our souls appease.
In understanding, we shall find,
A world of peace forever bind.

Blossoms of Vulnerability

In petals soft, our fears unfold,
Each bloom a story, brave and bold.
With every tear, a chance to grow,
In tender light, our spirits glow.

To share our hearts, a daring feat,
In gentle whispers, life's heartbeat.
As blossoms sway in the spring's embrace,
We find the strength to show our face.

In quiet moments, truths revealed,
The power of a heart unsealed.
With every sigh, we breathe in trust,
In the fragile, we find what's just.

Let roots entwine in rich, dark soil,
Where love can flourish through the toil.
In openness, we rise and stand,
With blooming hope, we'll touch the land.

So let us cherish every flower,
In vulnerability, we find power.
In this garden, may we discover,
The beauty found in one another.

Frames of Forgiveness

In shadows deep where sorrows dwell,
The heart learns softly, it has to tell.
With every tear, a lesson gained,
Forgiveness blooms where love remained.

Through open arms, the past can fade,
Embracing truth, the heart's cascade.
Layers peeled with tender care,
In gentle whispers, we repair.

The mirror shows the flaws we hide,
But kindness speaks, it won't divide.
In shattered frames, new stories weave,
Forgiveness paints what we believe.

Let time be soft, let healing stay,
In morning's light, the dark gives way.
To rise anew, from ashes gray,
In frames of love, we find our way.

The Language of Shared Glances

Behind closed doors where secrets breathe,
Two souls connect, a silent wreath.
In fleeting looks, a world crafted,
A dance unspoken, hearts are drafted.

A gentle smile, a knowing nod,
In crowded rooms, against the odd.
With every gaze, a bridge appears,
Echoes of laughter, shadows of tears.

Words left unsaid, but understood,
A tapestry of moments good.
In those brief ties, a bond is born,
The language shared, no heart can scorn.

Through eyes that speak, and hearts that know,
We weave a tale that only we show.
In a world so vast, yet so confined,
In shared glances, our souls aligned.

Beneath the Moonlit Promise

The silver glow on tranquil tides,
Whispers soft where hope resides.
Beneath the stars, our dreams ignite,
In moonlit beams, the shadows light.

Promises made in quiet grace,
Reflected in your gentle face.
The night unfolds, a sacred space,
Where every heartbeat finds its place.

With every breath, the universe speaks,
In silent words, our spirit seeks.
Together we bask, fear laid to rest,
In moonlit promise, we are blessed.

The world fades, just you and I,
Under the vast, embracing sky.
In this stillness, love reveals,
Beneath the moon, our heart it heals.

The Colors of Vulnerability

In hues of heartache, pain takes flight,
A canvas raw, emotions bright.
Courage blooms in every tear,
In colors bold, we face our fear.

Each stroke a story, each shade a truth,
In the palette of lessons learned in youth.
Fragile yet fierce, we stand exposed,
In vibrant tones, our spirit grows.

To open wide, let shadows blend,
In the spectrum's warmth, our hearts amend.
With every shade, a tale unfolds,
In vulnerability, we dare be bold.

The colors show what hearts can't say,
In tender strokes, they light the way.
For in the art of being real,
The colors of love, we learn to feel.

The Map of Our Embrace

In twilight's soft and gentle glow,
We trace the paths where memories flow.
Your hand in mine, we wander free,
Lost in the map of you and me.

Each breath a marker, each laugh a line,
Drawing the borders of love divine.
Through valleys deep and mountains high,
We carve our dreams beneath the sky.

The compass spins with every kiss,
Navigating a world of bliss.
With every turn, our spirits soar,
A journey etched forevermore.

Our footprints blend in sands of time,
Together forging our perfect rhyme.
In every hug, a secret space,
The treasure lies within our embrace.

So let the stars our way illuminate,
As we explore this love, our fate.
In every heartbeat, maps unfold,
In your arms, the world feels bold.

Fleeting Moments of Clarity

In whispers soft, the truth appears,
A flash of light that calms our fears.
In fleeting moments, clarity calls,
A glimpse of life beyond the walls.

The world spins fast, yet we stand still,
In sacred silence, we find our will.
The chaos fades, the noise subsides,
In these brief pauses, love abides.

With every breath, we touch the sky,
As worries fade and dreams comply.
In simple joys, we find our way,
With open hearts, we seize the day.

Through twilight hues, our spirits dance,
In every moment, there's a chance.
To hold onto what truly stays,
Amidst the fleeting, love always plays.

So gaze into the depths of time,
And let the heart's sweet echoes chime.
In these glimpses, truth reveals,
The quiet strength that love conceals.

A Knot Tied with Hope

In threads of fate, we weave our dreams,
A knot tied tight with hopeful seams.
Each twist a promise, each turn a grace,
In the tapestry of our embrace.

With every knot, we face the storm,
Creating shelter, keeping warm.
In tangled times, trust holds us fast,
A bond so strong, forever cast.

Among the trials, our hearts unite,
With every struggle, fueled by light.
In woven strength, our love will shine,
A masterpiece that's truly divine.

So let the winds of change blow wild,
Together we stand, love's faithful child.
For in this knot, our hopes entwine,
A future bright, forever thine.

In harmony, our stories blend,
With every thread, the tale won't end.
Hand in hand, we won't let go,
A knot tied deep with hope aglow.

The Symphony of Heartbeats

In rhythm soft, our heartbeats play,
A symphony that lights the way.
Each pulse a note, in perfect tune,
Together dancing beneath the moon.

With every thrum, a tender sound,
In this embrace, our love's profound.
The world may fade, yet we remain,
In melodies that ease the pain.

Notes of laughter, whispers sweet,
Composing joy in every beat.
In ebb and flow, our spirits rise,
Entwined in music, love never dies.

So let the millions of stars align,
As we create our own design.
In the symphony, we find our peace,
In every glance, our hearts' release.

With every heartbeat, futures blend,
As stories told, our souls ascend.
In harmony, we celebrate,
A timeless love that won't abate.

Unraveled Threads of Connection

In the tapestry of life, we weave,
Threads of laughter, threads of grief.
Each connection precious, yet frail,
Stories shared, like a gentle hail.

Time can fray the bonds we hold,
Yet memories shimmer, bright and bold.
Through distance, love can still be near,
In whispered secrets, loud and clear.

We search for meaning in the weave,
In every thread, we dare believe.
Together we stand, though apart we roam,
The heart's connection, a sacred home.

As stitches loosen, we learn to mend,
Life's design evolves, will not end.
With every knot, a lesson found,
In every heart, a love profound.

So cherish each thread, both weak and strong,
In this grand weave, we all belong.
Together we rise, together we fall,
Unraveled threads, yet we are all.

Navigating the Waters of Emotion

In the tides of feeling, we drift and sway,
Waves of joy, then shadows gray.
Hearts like vessels, set to roam,
Searching for solace, a place called home.

Some days a storm, fierce and wild,
Other days gentle, like a child.
Love's currents pull, both deep and wide,
In silent waters, we confide.

An anchor of hope, we seek to find,
To steady the ship, calm the mind.
Emotions rise, then ebb away,
In stillness, we learn, in chaos, we pray.

Navigating through waves of doubt,
Finding the light when the waters shout.
Trust in the journey, the paths we make,
Through turbulent seas, hearts won't break.

For every tear, there's laughter too,
Navigating waters, me and you.
Together we weather, together we fight,
In the vast ocean of day and night.

The Balance of Give and Take

In each exchange, we find our way,
A dance of hearts, a gentle sway.
To give is grace, to take is trust,
In this balance, love is a must.

A hand to hold, a shoulder near,
In moments shared, our path seems clear.
Life's rich lessons, whispered low,
In giving and taking, our spirits grow.

Yet tread with care upon this line,
Too much of either can turn malign.
An open heart, a listening ear,
Together we thrive, with love sincere.

When burdens heavy, share the load,
On this journey, we walk the road.
The beauty of balance, a sacred art,
In every flow, a dancing heart.

So in this life, let's find our grace,
In ebb and flow, we find our place.
Through give and take, a bond we form,
In harmony's wake, we feel the warm.

Blossoms of Resilience

In the garden where dreams take flight,
Resilience blooms, a radiant sight.
Though storms may rage and shadows fall,
Stronger we rise, we'll never stall.

Petals embrace the morning dew,
In every challenge, a chance anew.
Roots burrow deep in the earth's embrace,
In trials faced, we find our grace.

The sun will shine after the rain,
Through every struggle, grows the gain.
In colors bright, our spirits soar,
From cracks in the pavement, we'll learn to explore.

With every bloom, a story told,
Of courage found, of hearts so bold.
From the depths of sorrow, we cultivate,
Beauty emerges, we celebrate.

So let us tend to our inner field,
In love and strength, our hearts will yield.
Together we flourish, through life's intent,
In blossoms of resilience, our souls are bent.

An Open Book of Affections

Pages turn with gentle grace,
Whispers linger in each space.
Ink of love flows deep and true,
Every word a piece of you.

Memories dance across the sheets,
Moments captured, heart it beats.
Joy and sorrow intertwine,
In the margins, your hand in mine.

Chapters filled with laughter's light,
Dreams that spark in velvet night.
Through the storms and sunny skies,
Our story grows, it never dies.

Ink and paper hold our tales,
Bound by love that never pales.
Each new line a step we take,
In this book, we'll never break.

So let us write with passion's fire,
An open book, our hearts' desire.
With every word, the truth we scribe,
In timeless love, we shall describe.

In the Shadow of Sacrifice

Silent echoes fill the night,
Where shadows dwell, fading light.
Every choice a heavy weight,
Carved in pain, sealed by fate.

Hearts entwined with threads of gold,
Stories shared, but seldom told.
In the silence, we feel the cost,
Of love gained, but not without loss.

Beneath the stars, we stand so still,
In the quiet, we find our will.
Moments lost, yet never gone,
In our hearts, a brighter dawn.

The path we walk, both dark and bright,
Through every tear, a spark ignites.
For in this bond, we find our home,
In sacrifice, we'll never roam.

So here we stand, hand in hand,
In the shadow, we make our stand.
Through wounded hearts and endless night,
In love's embrace, we find the light.

From Strangers to Soulmates

Two wandering souls in the night,
Paths entwined, a fateful sight.
Eyes that meet, a spark ignites,
From strangers born, love takes flight.

Conversations flow like a stream,
Shared laughter, a waking dream.
In the silence, we understand,
The language spoken heart to hand.

Hands once empty, now entwined,
In the warmth, our hearts aligned.
With every step, we grow more sure,
This journey shared, a love so pure.

From simple glances, to deep embrace,
Time slows down in this sacred space.
What started small now fills the air,
From strangers found, to love we share.

So here we stand, the world our stage,
Writing our story on every page.
From quiet beginnings, we break the mold,
Two hearts united, a love untold.

The Mirror of Our Tomorrows

In the glass, reflections gleam,
A future built from shared dreams.
Every hope, a light that glows,
In the mirror, our love shows.

Through every trial, through every test,
We'll find our way, we'll be our best.
With open hearts, we chase the dawn,
In this journey, we go on.

The whispers of what's yet to be,
Echo softly, just you and me.
In every smile, in every tear,
The mirror whispers, "Love is near."

So let us dance, the shadows fade,
In this moment, memories made.
With every glance, our dreams align,
In the mirror's truth, your hand in mine.

As we paint the canvas wide,
Creating worlds, with love as guide.
In this glass, see what we'll find,
The mirror of our tomorrows, kind.

The Wisdom in Our Wounds

In every scar a story lies,
A testament to battles fought.
The pain, once sharp, now slowly dies,
Yet leaves a lesson deeply sought.

Through darkest nights we learn to grow,
Embracing every tear we shed.
In fragile hearts, true strength will show,
From shadows cast, our light is bred.

With time, we see the beauty born,
A tapestry of scars entwined.
In every heart that once was torn,
A wiser soul, we learn to find.

So hold your wounds with gentle grace,
For in their depths, the truth resides.
The wisdom found in each embrace,
Guides us as life's river glides.

For healing's path is not in vain,
But leads to shores of hope and trust.
In every loss, we find the gain,
Embracing life; we rise from dust.

Colors on a Canvas of Affection

Brush strokes dance in vibrant hues,
Each palette whispers tales of love.
From gentle pastels to bold cues,
Hearts flutter like the wings of doves.

Joy spills in crimson, bright and free,
While blues evoke a calm embrace.
Greens of growth, like whispered trees,
In every shade, a warm trace.

Together, we create a scene,
A masterpiece, our hearts aligned.
With every layer, moments glean,
In colors shared, two souls combined.

As sunlight warms the canvas wide,
Our laughter paints the air with glee.
In this creation, hearts abide,
We find forever's harmony.

So let us mix our tones each day,
A vibrant dance, our lives entwined.
In every brush, love's sweet ballet,
A canvas pure, our hearts enshrined.

In Storms We Find Our Light

When thunder roars and shadows creep,
We lift our heads to skies aflame.
In raging winds, our spirits leap,
Transforming fear to quiet fame.

Raindrops fall like whispered tales,
Each drop a chance to start anew.
In tempest's grip, our courage sails,
To find the strength to push right through.

As lightning crackles in the dark,
We glimpse the spark of inner fire.
With every blow, we leave a mark,
Defiance born from heart's desire.

Through fog and fury, shadows blend,
We navigate the paths so tight.
When storms arise, we shall not bend,
For in these trials, shines our light.

So let the thunder clap and roar,
We stand united, side by side.
In every storm, our spirits soar,
Together bold, in love, we stride.

The Warmth of a Steady Flame

In flickers soft, our hearts align,
A gentle glow that lights the night.
In whispered moments, love will shine,
Igniting dreams, we hold them tight.

A steady flame in darkest hours,
It warms the chill of doubt and fear.
Through stormy tides and blooming flowers,
Our love endures, forever near.

In each embrace, the fires rise,
An ember born from tender trust.
With every spark, a heart complies,
In warmth we find, our souls adjust.

As shadows dance around our feet,
We gather close, our spirits blend.
With steady hearts, no fear of defeat,
Together, love, our flames transcend.

So let the winds howl, let them rage,
Our steady flame will never wane.
In every chapter, every page,
We write our hearts, a warm refrain.

When Heartbeats Form a Language

In quiet rooms where shadows play,
A rhythm stirs, its soft ballet.
Each breath a note, each sigh a tune,
Together we dance beneath the moon.

Silent whispers through the night,
In heartbeat's pulse, we find our light.
Unspoken words weave in and out,
Love's secret song, without a doubt.

Fingers clasp, a gentle cling,
In shared moments, we find our spring.
Echoes linger in the air,
A melody only we can share.

Every glance, a silent plea,
In the union of you and me.
Harmony blooms where we reside,
In our hearts, the truth can't hide.

So let us dwell in this sweet space,
Where heartbeats form a soft embrace.
Connected threads of love and fate,
In rhythm's dance, we cultivate.

The Fabric of Togetherness

Threads of laughter, woven tight,
In the tapestry of day and night.
Each moment stitched with care and grace,
A vibrant hue in every place.

We gather memories, soft and rare,
In every glance, a silent prayer.
The fabric holds our stories tight,
Woven magic in shared delight.

Colors blend in rich embrace,
Each heartbeat finds its rightful space.
In the patterns, love's design,
An intricate weave, so divine.

In storms we weather, hand in hand,
Together we stand, a steadfast band.
The fabric breathes with dreams anew,
In every stitch, a love so true.

So let us cherish this woven thread,
The fabric of togetherness, widespread.
With every moment that we create,
We sew our hearts, we celebrate.

Within the Depths of Us

In the quiet, deep, we dwell,
Where stories whisper, hearts compel.
A world unseen, yet deeply felt,
Where shadows weave, and true bonds melt.

Through echoes of laughter and tears,
Within the depths, we face our fears.
Caverns rich with dreams and sighs,
Together we soar, we learn to rise.

Uncharted waters, vast and wide,
In the depths of us, we freely glide.
With every wave, a lesson learned,
In the silence, our spirits burned.

We navigate the tides that flow,
Together we find the depths we know.
With every turn, a deeper grace,
Within the depths, we find our place.

So let us wander, hand in hand,
Within the depths, where dreams expand.
In the stillness, our souls entwine,
In this sacred space, you are mine.

The Garden of Empathy

In the garden where feelings grow,
Seeds of kindness, we choose to sow.
Each act of love, a gentle breeze,
In the soil of hearts, we find our ease.

Blossoms bright, a fragrant air,
In shared burdens, we find our care.
Roots entwined in understanding,
A sacred bond, forever expanding.

Underneath the sun's warm glow,
The garden flourishes, helping sow.
Each flower speaks a silent truth,
In the blooms, we reclaim our youth.

Tending to each other's pain,
In the rain, compassion's gain.
Through seasons change, we still remain,
In the garden's heart, love's refrain.

So let us cherish this sacred ground,
Where empathy thrives, and hope is found.
In every petal, a lesson waits,
In the garden of empathy, love creates.

Fragments of a Forgotten Dream

In the stillness, whispers fade,
Shadows dance where hopes once played.
Memories linger, soft and slight,
Fragments lost in endless night.

Glimmers of joy, like stars, they twinkle,
Fleeting glimpses that make hearts crinkle.
A tapestry woven with golden threads,
In the silence, where lost feels led.

Through the veil, a soft light gleams,
Waking echoes of forgotten dreams.
In the corners of a slumbered mind,
Whispers of what we hoped to find.

Yet, as dawn breaks across the sky,
The timid shadows seem to sigh.
Holding tight to what has been,
In every pulse, in every dream.

Each fragment tells a tale anew,
Of laughter shared and sorrows too.
In the heart, where stories play,
Forgotten dreams still find their way.

The Map of Our Journey

In the weave of roads we tread,
Paths converge, as words are said.
With every step, a story spun,
A map of moments, one by one.

Mountains climbed and rivers crossed,
Lessons learned, though time is lost.
Each twist and turn, a place to grow,
The seeds of us in every flow.

Through valleys low and skies of gray,
Together we forged our own way.
Holding hands as clouds drift by,
The compass points to endless sky.

Winds may shift, and storms may swell,
Yet in your heart, I know so well.
No distance large, nor journey long,
In your presence, I feel so strong.

With ink of love, we chart our fate,
The map of us, it won't be late.
Each landmark shines, a memory bright,
Guiding us through the longest night.

When Time Stood Still

In a moment, the world paused,
Colors bright, and silence caused.
Time suspended, heartbeats sync,
Caught in magic, we barely blink.

A glance exchanged, our hands align,
In your eyes, the stars align.
No minutes passed, nor hours flown,
In that stillness, love was grown.

The air held secrets, soft and sweet,
A timeless dance on whispered feet.
Every breath, a promise made,
In that instant, fears would fade.

Boundless dreams in the twilight glow,
A universe for us to know.
In the silence, we found our song,
In that moment, where we belong.

As clocks resumed their steady chime,
I held your heart, you held my time.
Forever changed, our destinies sealed,
When time stood still, our love revealed.

Colors of Compassion

Canvas stretched, in vibrant hues,
Each brushstroke tells of love we choose.
Blues of calm, reds of fire,
In every shade, a spark of desire.

Greens of growth, and golds of light,
Coloring our world, pure and bright.
Compassion flows in every line,
Painting futures where hearts entwine.

With every color, we share our grace,
Forging connections in every space.
From gentle pastels to bold displays,
In our symphony, compassion stays.

The strokes of kindness free our soul,
Unfurling dreams, making us whole.
Together we create, hand in hand,
A masterpiece, forever planned.

In this gallery, we find our place,
Embracing life, with love's embrace.
Through every color, our journey flows,
In the heart of compassion, true love grows.

When Stars Align in Silence

In the quiet night sky, stars gleam,
Whispers of wishes float like a dream.
Hearts collide in a cosmic dance,
Fate unfolds with a fleeting glance.

Moonlight kisses the still, calm ground,
In this moment, true peace is found.
Voices hush, as shadows entwine,
When stars align, our souls combine.

Echoes of laughter, soft and rare,
In the dark, we breathe the same air.
Time stands still, wrapped in our light,
Lost together, two hearts in flight.

A gentle breeze carries our song,
In the silence, where we belong.
Cosmic wonders stretch far and wide,
When stars align, I'm by your side.

In dreams we wander, hand in hand,
Across the heavens, vast and grand.
Each twinkle tells stories unspoken,
In this silence, our hearts are open.

Beneath the Veil of Intimacy

In shadows cast by candlelight,
Whispers weave through the velvet night.
Eyes locked in a tender gaze,
In silence, love's warm embers blaze.

Words unspoken, yet deeply felt,
In a tender shelter, our hearts melt.
Every heartbeat, a secret shared,
In the stillness, we know we cared.

With each touch, a story unfolds,
Beneath the veil, our truth beholds.
In gentle caress, the world fades,
Wrapped in a warmth that never degrades.

Trust blooms softly, like morning dew,
In this haven, it's me and you.
Together we dance, a sacred rite,
Beneath the veil, hearts take flight.

Time drifts away, like a soft sigh,
In your embrace, I learn to fly.
With every breath, our spirits soar,
In this intimacy, we crave more.

So take my hand, let our hearts blend,
In this moment, our souls transcend.
Beneath the veil, forever remains,
An eternal bond that love sustains.

A Gentle Hand on Broken Dreams

In the quiet night, shadows fall,
Whispers of hope in the stillness call.
With a gentle hand, you mend the seams,
Reviving the echoes of broken dreams.

Each tear that falls tells a story true,
In your embrace, I find strength anew.
Pieces of past, scattered like dust,
In your warmth, I learn to trust.

Through the rubble, you clear a path,
Guiding me softly from sorrow's wrath.
A beacon of light in my darkest night,
You hold my heart, making it right.

Every sigh shared, a promise made,
In your presence, my fears start to fade.
Together we rise, like a brilliant dawn,
From broken dreams, new hopes are drawn.

With every word, you lift me higher,
A gentle hand, igniting the fire.
In the tapestry of love, we weave,
In our union, we learn to believe.

So let us chase those dreams once more,
With togetherness, the future we'll soar.
A gentle hand on this journey bright,
In the realm of dreams, we find our light.

The Ties That Bind Us

In laughter and tears, we stand so near,
Threads of our lives sewn with sincere.
With every moment, our bond grows tight,
In the tapestry of love, colors ignite.

Through trials faced and triumphs gained,
United we stand, through joy and pain.
The ties that bind us, strong and true,
In every heartbeat, I find you.

Hand in hand, we weather the storm,
In your embrace, I find my warm.
A dance of souls, so intricately wrought,
In every gesture, love is taught.

Time may challenge the paths we tread,
Yet through it all, our spirits are fed.
In the moments shared, no distance can sever,
The ties that bind us, now and forever.

With whispered dreams and visions grand,
We walk together through this land.
Every step taken, a promise rings,
In the love we share, the freedom it brings.

So let us cherish the way we shine,
In this journey, your heart is mine.
A symphony of souls, our spirits align,
In the ties that bind, our love will define.

The Garden of Forgiveness

In the quiet shade, hearts can mend,
Whispers of peace, a gentle blend.
Flowers bloom with colors bright,
Each petal soft, banishing night.

Under the arch of the old oak tree,
Roots dig deep, setting us free.
With every tear, a seed is sown,
In this garden, love has grown.

Sunlight dances on the dew,
Hope rises fresh with each new hue.
Forgiveness wraps like tender vines,
In every heart, a truth aligns.

The breeze carries soft, sweet songs,
Righting the places where we were wrong.
Paths converge, shadows fade,
In this sanctuary, peace is made.

Leaves whisper softly, secrets unfold,
Stories of courage, softly told.
In the garden, we find our grace,
Hand in hand, we claim our place.

Waiting for the Moonlight

Stars blink softly in the night,
Echoes of dreams take their flight.
Whispers of hope fill the air,
In this stillness, we lay bare.

Time ticks slowly, shadows play,
Anticipation lights the way.
With every breath, a story's spun,
Chasing the glow of the coming one.

The world is hushed, wrapped in dark,
A glimmer waits to leave its mark.
I sit with patience, heart in tune,
Yearning for the face of the moon.

Clouds drift lazily, soft and white,
Covering paths, hiding light.
But I believe in the dawn's return,
For in the waiting, there's much to learn.

Moments pass, the night grows deep,
In dreams, I wander, in silence, I weep.
Yet deep inside, a fire glows,
For soon, the silver light will pose.

And when it beams through the silent trees,
The world awakens, hearts feel ease.
In that glow, fears all take flight,
Together we'll dance in the moonlight.

Silhouettes of Shared Moments

Under the stars, shadows play,
Whispers of laughter fill the sway.
Hand in hand, we chase the night,
Creating tales woven tight.

In the fading light, silhouettes gleam,
Carving our place inside a dream.
Every glance holds stories vast,
Moments captured, never past.

Time flows gently like a stream,
Connected hearts weave a beam.
Steps taken, side by side,
In every heartbeat, love's abide.

With every breath, memories twine,
In the tapestry of moments divine.
Strength in silence, power in grace,
Our silhouettes time can't erase.

As dawn breaks with its tender hue,
Canvas of life painted anew.
In every sunrise, shadows fade,
But what we shared will never jade.

Lessons Written in the Stars

In the vast sky, secrets unfold,
Ancient stories whispered bold.
Stars align with a gentle hand,
Guiding our dreams, a cosmic band.

Each twinkle a lesson, precious and true,
Reminders of paths meant just for you.
Through trials faced and choices made,
In the starlight, fears will fade.

Look up high, let your spirit soar,
For within the night, there's so much more.
Celestial bodies dance and weave,
Teaching us how to believe.

In constellations, wisdom is cast,
Carved in the heavens, a spell is fast.
With every glance, let your heart feel,
In the universe, you're part of the reel.

So under the night, embrace your scars,
For you're a story written in stars.
Every heartbeat a note in the tune,
A melody sung under the moon.

Love's Geometry of Trust

In the angles where our hearts meet,
A steady line draws us near.
With each promise, we entreat,
Building bridges without fear.

Circles of warmth in our embrace,
Quadrants of laughter shared so free.
In every moment, we find grace,
Drawing paths for you and me.

Through the vertices of our dreams,
We sketch the future, bold and bright.
In perfect harmony, it seems,
Our love's design is pure delight.

Angles sharp, yet softly bend,
In every curve, our hearts relate.
Trust is the line that will not end,
In the geometry we create.

Together, we form a strong base,
With each step, we align in kind.
In the art of love, we find our place,
Two shapes entwined, forever defined.

Embracing the Unseen

In twilight's hush, we sense the veils,
Where shadows dance and whispers call.
Between the known, the heart prevails,
In the silence, love can sprawl.

The gentle breeze that strokes our skin,
Signs of promises yet to bloom.
In depths where every fear has been,
We find solace, breaking gloom.

Thoughts unspoken, glances exchanged,
Filling voids where words fall short.
In the spaces where hearts have ranged,
Lives unfold a sacred court.

What's unseen guides us through the night,
With faith as the lantern we hold.
In trust, we find our inner light,
And in our hearts, the stories told.

So let us hold this mystery dear,
With open arms, we embrace change.
For in the unseen, love is clear,
A bond unbroken, wide and strange.

Notes from a Devoted Heart

Each heartbeat writes a melody,
A symphony of love's sweet song.
With every note, you set me free,
In rhythms where we both belong.

Your laughter rings like chimes of gold,
A gentle echo in my mind.
In whispers soft, our tales unfold,
In every pause, a love defined.

The verses dance between our souls,
In stanzas woven rich and deep.
In love's embrace, we reach our goals,
A promise held in dreams we keep.

Though time may test our boundless trust,
Each line we write will bind us tight.
With patience, passion, and the dust,
Of memories, our hearts ignite.

So take this note, forever penned,
A testament to love's pure art.
In every phrase, our lives extend,
These notes from my devoted heart.

The Dance of Two Souls

In twilight's glow, we find our way,
Two souls entwined, a graceful sight.
With every step, our hearts will sway,
As stars adorn the velvet night.

The music plays, a soft refrain,
In harmony, we twirl and spin.
With you, I lose all sense of pain,
In this rhythm, we begin.

Footprints etched in time's embrace,
A tapestry of love defined.
Each gaze exchanged, we find our place,
In this dance, our lives aligned.

As seasons change, we won't let go,
Through storms and calm, we move as one.
In trust, we find our steady flow,
A dance that's just begun.

So let the world fade from our sight,
In this moment, let's lose control.
For in your arms, it feels so right,
Together, we're the dance of souls.

Chasing Rainbows Through Tears

In the storm, colors blend bright,
Each drop a reminder of light.
Through the mist, hopes we find,
Echoes of dreams left behind.

With every tear that we shed,
A promise of joy lies ahead.
Chasing rainbows, we learn to see,
The beauty in pain, setting us free.

Fragments of laughter in sorrow,
We dare to believe in tomorrow.
In the sky, our spirits soar,
As we chase what we long for.

The paths may twist, the shadows roam,
With every step, we forge a home.
Through rain and shine, we'll always chase,
The vibrant hues that life can place.

So let the world spin around,
In tears, our true selves are found.
Chasing rainbows, hearts aligned,
In the tapestry of love, we're entwined.

The Silent Conversation

Across the room, our eyes connect,
In silence, we share, we reflect.
Words unspoken, yet so loud,
In the quiet, we're truly proud.

A glance that says more than a page,
In each heartbeat, a hidden sage.
Time stands still as we embrace,
In the glimmer of a shared space.

The world may fade, but we remain,
In this moment, there's no pain.
A whisper held in a single gaze,
In our silence, we set ablaze.

Lamp light flickers, shadows play,
Navigating what words can't say.
In this dance, we find the key,
Unlocking depths of mystery.

So let the silence sing its song,
In this stillness, we belong.
The language of the heart defined,
In silent conversations intertwined.

Love's Little Charades

In playful glances, we disguise,
The truth behind our wandering eyes.
Each smile a hint, a sweet facade,
In love's charades, we play our card.

With every laugh, a tale is spun,
In this game, we're all but one.
Fleeting moments, wrapped in cheer,
Hidden meanings, drawing near.

A gentle touch, a fleeting stare,
We dance around what we both share.
In the chaos, we find our way,
Through love's charades, we choose to play.

The world watches, unaware of bliss,
In these charades, there's magic in the kiss.
Every heartbeat, a secret told,
In love's embrace, we're brave and bold.

So let the game continue on,
In our hearts, the spark's never gone.
With playful smiles, we keep the score,
In love's little charades, we want more.

Moments Captured in Time

Fleeting seconds, a blink away,
In snapshots, memories sway.
Each smile held, a frame so dear,
Moments captured, crystal clear.

The laughter shared beneath the sun,
In quiet corners, joy we've won.
In every glance, a story's told,
Moments of warmth against the cold.

Time may pass, a river flows,
Yet in our hearts, the memory glows.
In stillness found in a busy life,
Moments bloom amidst the strife.

So let us pause in this embrace,
In memories, we find our place.
Forever cherished, never lost,
Moments captured, worth the cost.

Together we'll weave through the years,
In laughter, love, and sometimes tears.
Moments captured in a heart's rhyme,
Eternal, we dance through time.

Dancing Through the Rain

Raindrops fall like gentle notes,
In a song that's yet to be sung.
Under gray skies, we learn to float,
Joy arises where hearts are young.

With each splash, our worries cease,
We twirl and spin, a freedom found.
Nature's rhythm brings us peace,
In puddles deep, we dance unbound.

The world blurs, a watercolor,
Colors blend, entwined as one.
In this moment, we discover,
Love's sweet embrace, two souls as one.

Laughing loud, we don't feel cold,
The rain becomes our muse tonight.
In the storm, our hearts grow bold,
Together, we find our light.

So let it pour; let shadows play,
We'll find magic in the gray.
Dancing through the rain, we fly,
In water's kiss, we touch the sky.

Whispers of the Heart's Wisdom

In silent moments, secrets bloom,
A gentle nudge, a soft embrace.
Heart speaks freely, dispelling gloom,
Words of comfort, a sacred space.

Listen close to the truth within,
Intuition guides our way forward.
A beating drum where love begins,
In every heartbeat, wisdom poured.

Whispers float on the evening air,
Soft like petals, sweet like song.
Every flutter shows that we care,
In this dance, we both belong.

Trust the path that you choose to tread,
Let your heart lead, let it be free.
With each step, new visions spread,
In the stillness, we find the key.

As dawn breaks, new stories wake,
With love's language, we shall find,
All the pieces that life can make,
In whispers, the heart is kind.

Echoes of Affection

In quiet rooms where shadows play,
Affection lingers in the air.
Softly spoken, they gently sway,
Carried whispers, a lover's prayer.

Moments shared, they flicker bright,
Like fireflies on a summer's eve.
In every glance, a spark ignites,
With every word, we learn to believe.

Together we build, brick by brick,
A fortress strong, a home of trust.
In laughter's echo, time feels quick,
Affinity grows, forever just.

The warmth of touch, the depth of gaze,
In simple acts, our hearts entwine.
Celebrating love in myriad ways,
In every heartbeat, your soul mine.

In echoes soft, our stories weave,
Threads of joy and gentle strife.
With each moment, we achieve,
A tapestry of our shared life.

The Art of Tender Understanding

In the silence, hearts converse,
In gentle gestures, feelings flow.
With patient minds, we softly traverse,
The depths of love, learning to know.

Embrace the flaws, the hidden parts,
A fragile beauty in each scar.
With tender hands and open hearts,
We can heal wounds, we can go far.

A shared glance, a knowing smile,
In quietude, we find our way.
With every step, we bridge the mile,
Together, we choose love each day.

In laughter and tears, we intertwine,
The art of understanding unfolds.
In each moment, emotions align,
Creating a story that forever holds.

So let us cherish this sweet dance,
With open hearts, we shall take flight.
In the art of love, we find our chance,
To embrace each day, to share our light.

Shadows of Past Embraces

In twilight's glow, memories sigh,
Whispers dance where shadows lie.
Echoes of laughter fill the air,
Fleeting moments, tender care.

The touch of warmth, now bittersweet,
Time stands still, the heart's repeat.
Frozen frames that softly fade,
Love's embrace in memories laid.

Lost in dreams, we softly tread,
Haunted paths where angels fled.
Each corner turned, a face we knew,
In every shadow, the past shines through.

Yet here we stand, hand in hand,
Together still, we make our stand.
Through shadows thick, we find our way,
In every dusk, there's light of day.

With every sigh, memories weave,
A tapestry of love, we believe.
Through echoes past, a future calls,
In shadows bright, our love enthralls.

The Language of Silence

In silent rooms, the heart speaks loud,
A gentle pulse, beneath the shroud.
Words unspoken, yet understood,
In quiet moments, life feels good.

Eyes that linger, souls entwined,
Finding strength in love defined.
A tender glance, a knowing smile,
Bridges built that span the miles.

Silence wraps us in its grace,
Time slows down in this embrace.
In every pause, a world unfolds,
In the quiet, our love molds.

We listen close to what's unseen,
In every heartbeat, a sacred dream.
Through the stillness, we are free,
In silence, whispers carry we.

So let us dwell in this sweet space,
Where every silence finds its place.
In the language few can hear,
Our hearts converse, forever near.

Reflections in a Loving Mirror

In the glass, our souls collide,
Reflections dance, love can't hide.
Every glance reveals a truth,
In mirrored depths, we find our youth.

Through time's lens, our lives appear,
Moments cherished, crystal clear.
The echoes of our laughter ring,
In timeless loops, our spirits sing.

With every wrinkle, stories share,
Adventures bold, joys laid bare.
In you, I see the light of dawn,
In your embrace, I am reborn.

Together framed in love's embrace,
A portrait drawn, a sacred space.
Through every season, we reflect,
In love's mirror, we connect.

So here we stand, entwined as one,
In the reflection of the sun.
In loving mirrors, truths unfold,
Our hearts the canvas, a story told.

Storms and Calm of Two Souls

When tempests roar, and shadows fall,
Together we rise, we heed the call.
In stormy seas, our anchors fast,
Through every wave, our love holds vast.

Thunder crashes, the skies do weep,
Yet in our hearts, a promise deep.
We dance through storms, hand in hand,
Finding solace in shifting sand.

In the calm that follows the fight,
We find our peace, our shared light.
Every struggle, a lesson learned,
In the calm, our passions burned.

With every gust that sweeps us near,
We face the winds, we shed the fear.
Together strong, we face the storm,
In unity, our hearts are warm.

Through every trial, we emerge anew,
In the calm, I find you true.
For in this life, come what may,
With storms and calm, our love will stay.

Rising from Heartbreak

In shadows deep, I found my light,
A tender spark ignites the night.
With every tear that stained my face,
I learned to rise and embrace grace.

From whispered dreams now far away,
Hope's gentle touch begins to play.
The heart once shattered starts to mend,
In healing's arms, I find a friend.

Through trials faced and lessons learned,
The fire within has brightly burned.
With every setback, strength I gain,
A tale of courage born from pain.

So here I stand, though bruised and scarred,
A warrior forged, my spirit starred.
Each heartbeat sings a brave new start,
From ashes rises a hopeful heart.

Pages of a Shared Story

In whispered words, our voices blend,
Each chapter penned, a tale to send.
With laughter shared and tears we shed,
A tapestry of life we spread.

Through seasons change, we write our fate,
With ink of dreams, we hesitate.
Through quiet nights and sunny days,
Our journey flows in many ways.

Each line a promise, each pause a sigh,
Together, under the vast sky.
From every page, a truth unfolds,
In love's warm grasp, a story holds.

The bookmarks placed in time's embrace,
Memories etched, a sacred space.
In every word, a heart we see,
A binding thread that sets us free.

So let us write, with hearts aglow,
The pages turn, as feelings flow.
In every sentence, we find our way,
A shared story, day by day.

Crumpled Letters and New Beginnings

In crumpled folds, words lie in wait,
A tale of love, a twist of fate.
Once penned with hope, now marked by pain,
Yet from these scars, new dreams can gain.

Ink smudged by the tears I cried,
Each letter holds a piece of pride.
In every crease, a lesson learned,
From ashes of the past, we've turned.

With fresh white sheets, I start anew,
Beneath the sky, a brighter hue.
The past may haunt but can't confine,
From crumpled letters, I will shine.

So fingertips dance across the page,
A story sparked, unlocked from cage.
In every word, a world reborn,
New beginnings rise with each dawn.

With courage found, I'll write today,
A future bright, come what may.
In crumpled letters, strength I find,
A heart renewed, a love that's kind.

The Symphony of Trust

In quiet notes, our hearts align,
A gentle rhythm, pure and fine.
Each glance exchanged, a silent song,
Together we feel where we belong.

Through highs and lows, we play our part,
A melody crafted from the heart.
In harmony, we find our way,
With every chord, come what may.

When doubts arise like stormy skies,
Our trust, a beacon that never dies.
In every struggle, hand in hand,
A symphony that understands.

With every beat, our spirits soar,
A dance of dreams, forevermore.
In whispered vows, we'll find the tune,
A love that blossoms, grows like June.

So let us play this sacred score,
With passion deep, we'll always more.
The symphony of us, a timeless art,
A masterpiece crafted by the heart.

A Voyage of the Heart

Across the ocean's deep blue,
Where dreams and whispers softly brew,
A compass set to guide the soul,
In love's embrace, we find our whole.

Like waves that dance upon the shore,
Our hearts entwined, forevermore,
Each heartbeat echoes through the night,
A journey filled with pure delight.

In starry skies our wishes soar,
With every tide, we seek to explore,
The depths of passion, fierce and bright,
Together chasing morning light.

Through storms that test our fragile fate,
We navigate with hope innate,
No distance great can tear apart,
The bond we share, a sacred art.

So hand in hand, we chart our course,
With love as wind, a gentle force,
A voyage endless, hearts set free,
In every heartbeat, you are me.

Pathways of Passion

Through tangled woods where shadows play,
We wander timeless, night and day,
Each path a twist of fate's design,
Your heart in tune, forever mine.

The scent of roses fills the air,
A fleeting glance, a loving stare,
With every step, the world awakes,
In whispered dreams, the spirit shakes.

We chase the sun, we race the moon,
With every heartbeat, love's sweet tune,
In laughter shared, in silence found,
Together lost, together bound.

Across the hills, through valleys wide,
Our passion glows like morning tide,
In every sigh, in every kiss,
We find our truth, eternal bliss.

So let us roam where hearts can soar,
In pathways rich with love's allure,
With every turn, we claim our fate,
In passion's arms, we celebrate.

The Silence Between Us

In quiet nights where stillness reigns,
We share a bond, though no words chain,
The space that flickers, soft and bright,
In whispered breaths, we feel the light.

Between the lines of what we say,
A symphony in silence play,
Your gaze, a language rich and pure,
In every tense, a love that's sure.

The moments stretch, a tender thread,
In pauses long, our hearts are fed,
With every heartbeat, time stands still,
Together lost, in quiet thrill.

Though silence reigns, our spirits speak,
In knowing smiles, in touches sleek,
A world unseen between our souls,
In cherished notes, our love consoles.

So let the world fade into gray,
In silence, we shall find our way,
For in the peace of what we share,
Lies every dream, our answered prayer.

Breaths of Surrender

In twilight's glow, we find our peace,
With every breath, the worries cease,
In gentle waves, our spirits blend,
A tranquil space where love won't end.

To close the eyes and feel your heart,
In tender moments, never part,
The world beyond fades from the view,
In sweet surrender, just us two.

With whispers soft, like leaves in fall,
We dance together, hear the call,
To lose ourselves in time and space,
In every breath, a warm embrace.

Let go of fears, let anger fade,
In love's warm light, we're unafraid,
For in your arms, I find my way,
A breath of hope, come what may.

So linger long, let moments flow,
In breaths of surrender, warmth we know,
Together, always intertwined,
In love's sweet song, our hearts aligned.

Finding Harmony in Dissonance

In chaos, we dance, a wild refrain,
Notes clash and collide, yet beauty remains.
Through discord we seek a melody new,
A harmony formed, where shadows break through.

Whispers of thunder, a tempest so loud,
Underneath the chaos, feelings unbowed.
We learn to embrace all that we loose,
Finding our voices, together we choose.

In struggles, we find the strength to unite,
Dissonant notes transform into light.
Melodies stitched from fragments of pain,
Building a symphony, love's sweet domain.

No longer afraid of a world torn apart,
In the dissonance, we find a new heart.
From the ashes of silence, we rise and ascend,
In every note, there lies hope to mend.

So let us combine our colors and sound,
In every discord, true beauty is found.
Together we'll sing, a future we seek,
In the dance of our hearts, we flourish and speak.

The Solace of Hand in Hand

In gentle embrace, we find our way clear,
Through trials and tempest, we share every tear.
With hands intertwined, our fears are in flight,
Together, we shine through the dark of the night.

Each step that we take, both shaky and small,
Together we rise, we will never fall.
In laughter and sorrow, we weave every thread,
The tapestry formed holds the words left unsaid.

Our hearts are a compass, guiding us true,
Through valleys of shadows, to skies ever blue.
With faith in each other, we bravely will stand,
The solace we find in the warmth of hand.

In quiet moments, just feeling the beat,
The world fades away, with love that's complete.
Each touch is a promise, a vow that's so grand,
In this dance of life, together we stand.

So take my hand, let us wander untamed,
In the garden of dreams, our hearts remain claimed.
Through storms and through sunshine, we'll journey on,
In the solace of hand in hand, we're reborn.

Seeds of Change in Our Hearts

In the soil of our souls, we plant tiny seeds,
Hopes blossoming bright, fulfilling our needs.
With nurturing care, they reach for the skies,
Transforming our lives, as we learn to rise.

Through seasons of doubt, storms threaten to sway,
But roots grow much deeper, come what may.
With patience, we wait as the moments unfold,
In the garden of change, new stories are told.

Each seed that we sow brings a chance to renew,
In the warmth of our voices, we find strength anew.
Through laughter and tears, we gather the rain,
Nurturing dreams through the joy and the pain.

Together we stand, in the light of our truth,
Embracing the wisdom that flowers in youth.
The seeds of our hearts, they bloom and expand,
Creating a world where love gives a hand.

So let us unite, and water this ground,
For the seeds of change in our hearts can be found.
We'll cultivate hope, hand in hand we'll embrace,
In this garden of life, together, we'll grace.

The Strength of Fragile Bonds

In whispers, we find the courage to speak,
Fragile threads woven, but never too weak.
In moments of silence, connections ignite,
A tapestry strong, yet tender and light.

Through laughter we gather, through trials we grow,
In the arms of each other, we learn to let go.
These bonds that may tremble, yet steadfastly stand,
With care and compassion, forever we'll band.

In the warmth of a smile, in the touch of a hand,
The strength of our bonds is a love that will stand.
In shadows and sunshine, we'll dance all the same,
Through seasons of change, we'll hold onto flame.

Fragility teaches us where to be bold,
To cherish and value the stories we hold.
Each thread may be fragile, yet woven with grace,
In life's grand design, we each find our place.

So let us embrace what makes us feel whole,
Through love, through connection, we all share a role.
In the strength of our fragile, unbreakable bonds,
We navigate life, where true heart always responds.

Fleeting Echoes of Emotion

Whispers in the night air,
Memories softly fade.
Each laugh that we shared,
An impression that's made.

The tears that we've shed,
Mark moments we hold dear.
In shadows, they linger,
Yet vanish with the fear.

A glance in the mirror,
Reflections of the past.
What once felt eternal,
Is fading too fast.

In the silence that follows,
Emotions take flight.
Fleeting, yet timeless,
They dance in the night.

With every heartbeat's echo,
A story unfolds.
The fleeting nature of feelings,
Is a treasure to hold.

Yet as days grow longer,
And memories entwine,
The echoes of our hearts,
Forever align.

Roots of Enduring Warmth

In the garden of our hearts,
Quiet roots take hold.
Through storms and shifting sands,
Our bond will not fold.

Beneath the surface lies,
A love deep and profound.
Together we weather,
The trials that abound.

Branches reach for the sky,
In search of the light.
With patience and nurture,
Our spirits take flight.

The seasons may change,
But warmth stays the same.
Each hug and each smile,
Are whispers of flame.

Strong roots, they remind us,
Of where we belong.
In the heart of our garden,
We thrive, brave and strong.

A Tapestry Woven in Time

Threads of gold and silver,
Interlace in our tale.
Each moment a pattern,
In the vast, woven whale.

Colors blend and shimmer,
Stories pushed and pulled.
A tapestry of memories,
In our hearts, forever mulled.

Stitches of laughter,
And tears that we've dropped.
Each knot a reminder,
Of the love that can't stop.

Through the ages we'll travel,
Each color a phase.
Together we craft,
An exquisite gaze.

Woven in the fabric,
A connection so fine.
In the heart of our journey,
Is a tapestry divine.

The Pillars of Shared Trust

Foundations built on whispers,
Solid as the stone.
Through trials we have weathered,
A bond that's fully grown.

Each promise like a pillar,
Stands steady and tall.
In shadows, we support,
We catch when we fall.

Integrity and honor,
Weaves between each thread.
With every honest word,
New levels we are fed.

The strength of shared trust,
Is a beacon of light.
Guiding us through darkness,
Our hearts shining bright.

In unity we flourish,
With courage we stand fast.
Together we rise high,
Our love built to last.

The Bridge of Understanding

In silence we weave thoughts anew,
Crossing divides, hearts steady and true.
Each word a step on a fragile span,
Building a bond, hand in hand we ran.

With patience, we tread on this path bright,
Finding the glow in the shade of night.
Two souls united, we learn to see,
The beauty that blooms in harmony.

Through storms and whispers, our voices soar,
Strength in connection, we rise evermore.
A tapestry rich, with colors entwined,
Reflecting the moments, our lives combined.

In laughter we find the keys to unlock,
The barriers fading, like tides on a rock.
Together we cherish the journey we make,
On this bridge of understanding, no breaks.

So step by step, let us travel along,
With hearts full of hope, forever strong.
For in this embrace, we learn to believe,
The bridge we have built, none will deceive.

Whispers across the Miles

In twilight's hush, your name I call,
Carried softly like leaves that fall.
A breeze that dances, a fleeting sigh,
Connecting us close, beneath vast sky.

Each letter penned, a gentle touch,
Words that linger, meaning so much.
Through nights so dark, stars light our way,
In whispers, I find you, come what may.

Time zones may part, but souls align,
Across the miles, our hearts entwine.
With echoes of dreams and hopes we share,
A bond unbroken, eternally rare.

Daylight will dim, but I will remain,
A faithful promise, like summer rain.
Distance may grow, but love won't fade,
In whispers serenading, memories made.

So here in silence, I send my plea,
To feel your essence, near to me.
For even in longing, the love is true,
In whispers across the miles, I find you.

Embracing the Uncertainty

In shadows of doubt, I find my way,
With courage to face the break of day.
Each step unpredictable, yet boldly made,
In uncertainty's arms, my fears start to fade.

The winds may change, and paths may curve,
But in each challenge, new strengths I serve.
Embracing the chaos, I learn to dance,
Finding my rhythm in each circumstance.

With open heart, I welcome the new,
In the unknown, I rediscover hue.
Though questions may rise like waves in the sea,
In this fertile ground, I'm wild and free.

Moments fleeting, yet rich with gold,
Tales yet untold gently unfold.
I cherish the journey, wherever it leads,
In the embrace of the uncertain, I plant my seeds.

So here I stand, unafraid to roam,
For in each stumble, I find my home.
With eyes wide open, I'll greet the storm,
Embracing the uncertainty, I am reborn.

Echoes of Laughter

In a room filled with light, laughter spills free,
Like ripples on water, it dances with glee.
Each chuckle a treasure, warm and bright,
Echoes of joy that soar into the night.

Memories crafted in moments so dear,
Laughter that lingers, a song to the ear.
Through highs and lows, it weaves us together,
A fabric of smiles that softens the weather.

In the stories we share, the humor unfolds,
Binding our hearts with threads made of gold.
Embracing the silly, the absurd, the fun,
With laughter as fuel, we can never be done.

Through trials and triumphs, it's always near,
An antidote sweet that washes our fear.
In the echoes we find the light of our past,
A melody cherished, a bond unsurpassed.

So let us relive every giggle and cheer,
In the echoes of laughter, we hold what is dear.
For life is a canvas, painted in glee,
In this symphony of laughter, we always will be.

Canvas of Uncharted Affection

Upon the canvas, colors blend,
Each stroke a whisper, hearts transcend.
Uncharted paths where dreams can flow,
In vibrant hues, our love shall grow.

Brushes touch, igniting the night,
With every shade, we chase the light.
In swirls of passion, we find our way,
Creating memories that forever stay.

Through swaths of blue, and crimson bright,
We paint emotions, pure delight.
Each canvas speaks of what we've known,
In uncharted realms, we are not alone.

As shadows dance upon the frame,
Our hearts entwined, we'll stake our claim.
For in this art, we find our grace,
In every line, a warm embrace.

So let us linger, brush in hand,
In silence, let our spirits stand.
For on this canvas, love takes flight,
In uncharted realms, we write our light.

Letters Written in Touch

Fingers trace the lines of fate,
A silent script, our hearts create.
With every touch, a letter sent,
In whispered words, our souls are bent.

In soft caress, we write our tale,
A gentle breeze where feelings sail.
In each embrace, a paragraph grows,
A novel sealed with tender prose.

Breathe in the ink of cherished dreams,
Where every moment flows like streams.
The stories linger, soft and sweet,
In every heartbeat, love's heartbeat.

So let our fingers gently blend,
In this letter, love won't end.
For in the closeness, we define,
A world where dreams and hearts align.

Through letters crafted by our touch,
We find the truth, we find so much.
Each page we turn, a new embrace,
In our love's book, a sacred space.

The Evolution of Togetherness

From two lone stars, to galaxies bright,
We weave our tales in the dark of night.
With time as thread, we spin and twine,
In the loom of fate, our hearts align.

From tangled roots, we grow and climb,
With every season, in perfect rhyme.
In storms we weather, in sunlit days,
Our love evolves in countless ways.

Through laughter's echo and sorrow's song,
We find our voice where we belong.
In every journey, side by side,
Together we learn, together we ride.

From whispers soft to shouts of cheer,
Each moment shared draws us near.
The evolution shines through the years,
A tapestry stitched with joys and tears.

So let us flourish, expand our view,
In this grand dance where love is true.
For in our hearts, together we'll be,
An ever-evolving tapestry.

Shadows of Love Drawn in Light

In twilight's glow, our shadows play,
Silhouettes dance in a dreamy sway.
With every heartbeat, they intertwine,
In love's soft shadows, our souls align.

Beneath the stars, whispers ignite,
Casting our hopes in the pale moonlight.
Shadows stretch longer with a sigh,
In this fleeting moment, we learn to fly.

As daylight fades, our shadows blend,
In twilight's embrace, we find a friend.
With hands entwined, we carve our way,
Through shades of passion, night turns to day.

For love is painted in hues so bright,
With shadows drawn in the softest light.
In lingering glances, secrets unfold,
In love's own story, endlessly told.

So let the shadows guide our flight,
As love grows bolder in the night.
With every touch, we sketch our part,
Shadows of love, a work of art.

Milton Keynes UK
Ingram Content Group UK Ltd.
UKHW021824311024
450535UK00010B/199